THE KATHLEEN PARTRIDGE SERIES

Kathleen Partridge's Book of Flowers
Kathleen Partridge's Book of Friendship
Kathleen Partridge's Book of Golden Thoughts
Kathleen Partridge's Book of Tranquil Moments

First published in Great Britain in 1997 by
Jarrold Publishing Ltd
Whitefriars, Norwich NR3 1TR

Designed and produced by Visual Image, Craigend, Brimley Hill,
Churchstanton, Taunton, Somerset TA3 7QH

Illustrations by Jane Watkins

Edited by Donald Greig

ISBN 0-7117-0904-1

Kathleen Partridge's
BOOK OF
Tranquil Moments

Kathleen Partridge

Only a Petal

Only a leaf in the morning dew
Or hole in the fence where a rose climbs through,
The song of the sea or the sunset's kiss
Life is worth living for this.

Only the smile of the child next door
Or news from a friend on a distant shore,
Though the rest of the day has gone amiss
Life is worth living for this.

Only a petal pale and pink
With memories sweet to form a link
With past or present times of bliss,
Life is worth living for this.

Glint of Gold

In every humdrum day
There is a little glint of gold
A purpose in the living
That is lovely to behold.

A reason for existence
In the dark – a glowing ember
That lights the dullest duty
With a moment to remember.

Remembering

Never a day runs to an end
Without some kindness from a friend,
Without remembering the name
Of one we love who stays the same.

To doubt the love of such a one
Would be to disbelieve the sun
A lack of faith, that stays awake
Doubting that the dawn will break.

Stepping-Stones

In the music of the morning
Where the shadows meet and blend
The water chases sunbeams
As it hurries to descend.

And so the world makes merry
With the green and golden tones
And the fretful fuss of living
Grows as smooth as stepping-stones.

Good Wishes
Through the Year

I wish for you good health in Spring,
When breezes from the sea are blowing,
And time and tide on life's high seas
Bring in your dream ships gaily glowing.

I wish for you a summer garden
Softly sheltered, gay with flowers,
A view from every window
To enhance the passing hours.

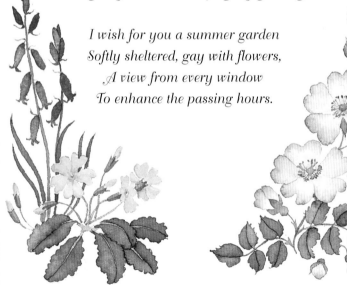

Happiness in Autumn
When the leaves are bronze and yellow
With matching memories
As calm and quiet, cool and mellow.

And in the Winter, may you have
Contentment and a cosy fire,
But most of all companionship
Most suited to your heart's desire.

Fledgling

He bursts his shell in Spring
And sets his song to nature's lilt,
His eyes will open to the view
Of blossoms over-split.

From ivy leaf to courtyard wall
From chimney-pot to glen,
He'll know the haunts of squirrels
As he knows the homes of men.

He'll see as much of Heaven
As he sees of mother earth,
These wonders are his heritage
Right from his hour of birth.

Wake up and Sing

High hills bring hopeful thoughts
And happy hearts make helpful deeds
Now is the time to gather flowers
Where friendship plants the seeds.

The time for looking up old friends
And going on the spree
For a trip along the river
Or an outing to the sea.

Our Dog

He is more than a pet, he is
more than a friend,
He's a reason for living on
which we depend;
With his head on one side and
his paw held aloft,
Our firmest reproval grows
suddenly soft;
He meets us, he greets us,
enslaved from the start,
When he nuzzles our hand as
he tugs at our heart.

Holiday Time

Leave the world of commerce
And let nature call the tune,
Idling in a haze
Of golden sand and tufted dune.

Brook no interruptions
In the sweet untroubled hours
And taste the morning fragrance
In the scent of many flowers.

And when the sky and ocean
Meet and blend in heavenly blue,
Then will the heart refreshed
Be as contented as the view.

Home to Friends

Laughter is like summer sunshine
When the day is born,
The heart's content is in the gold
That glorifies the dawn.

So when refreshing showers fall
And bathe the world with dew,
Then let me sing the day away
And let me laugh with you.

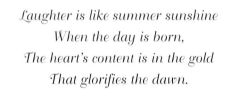

Time and Tide

Time and the flowing streams of life
Make changes on the earth around,
Villages emerge as towns
That were by old-world customs bound.

Trees spread or fall and rivers widen
Brooks run dry and forests grow,
We always find some changes
In the views we used to know.

Serenity

The flowers talk, yet do not need an answer,
The grasses sigh, and yet they are not sad,
The leaves are rustling one against the other
To tell of all the lovely days we've had.

There's so much movement that is never restless
And so much sound that does not interrupt,
The winds are whistling wisdom in the hedges
In tones that are not tiring, not abrupt.

And that is why the earth contains such solace
Harmonious to hear and cool to touch,
For nature has so many lovely voices,
And yet she never seems to talk too much.

Our Tree

May life for you be like this gracious tree
Rooted in strength and grown in majesty,
Defying storms, although it still achieves
To catch the sunlight filtering through the leaves.

This stately tree, as quiet as a psalm
Where birds may nestle in her knotted arm
And rest in safety, rocking as they trill
Surveying spire and mansion, vale and hill.

A shelter for the ones who come and go
At peace with God, good friends with those below,
Maturing wisely through each growing stage
Upright in youth and beautiful in age.

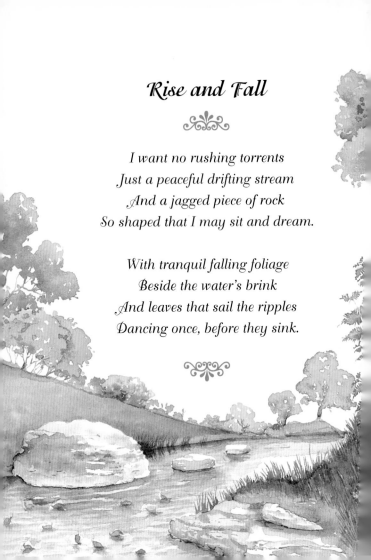

Rise and Fall

I want no rushing torrents
Just a peaceful drifting stream
And a jagged piece of rock
So shaped that I may sit and dream.

With tranquil falling foliage
Beside the water's brink
And leaves that sail the ripples
Dancing once, before they sink.

Growing Old

It is the Autumn of the year
That makes the harvest moon appear
To shine upon the glowing gold
Of lovely leaves now growing old.

And may the self-same beauty grace
The contours of a gentle face
That time has touched and left still fair
And shining with the kindness there.

Because of You

Can you say at close of day
Before you meet the night
Of all the troubles in the world
You helped to put one right?

That just one heart was happier
Because your smile was true,
One wrinkle in the folds of life
Was smoothed... because of you?